MIND RENEWAL
TRANSFORMATION DEVOTIONAL Vol. 2

Presented to

_____

By

_____

Date
_____

MIND RENEWAL TRANSFORMATION DEVOTIONAL Vol. 2

A 30-Day Transformational Journey

LEOSTONE MORRISON

Kingston, Jamaica W.I.

Copyright © 2020 by Leostone Morrison

ISBN-13: 978-1-62676-587-0

ALL RIGHTS RESERVED

Without limiting the rights under copyright reserved above, no part of this publication may be reproduced, stored in or introduced into a retrieval system, or transmitted, in any form, or by any means (electronic, mechanical, photocopying, recording, or otherwise), without the prior contractual or written permission of the copyright owner of this work.

. . . . .

Published by
Extra MILE Innovators
21 Phoenix Avenue,
Kingston 10, Jamaica W.I.
www.extramileja.com
administrator@extramileja.com
Tele: (1876) 782-9893

Ebook Cover Design by Tevaun Brown
tbartgraphic@gmail.com

Print Cover, Layout and Editing by the EMI Team

Unless otherwise stated Scripture verses are quoted from the New King James Version of the Bible

Author Contact

For consultation, feedback or speaking engagements contact the author at restorativeauthor@gmail.com

PRAISE FOR THE MIND RENEWAL DEVOTIONAL SERIES

I was only day eight in when I began to feel empowered. It was a great struggle to go back into my past to deal with circumstances and situations that were contributing to multiple blocks in my life. It was worth it to get to the place of a new mindset. Volume One did it for me. I now know the sky is really not the limit my–mind is.

Tamica Lestrade
Educator/Entrepreneur

These are inspirational, awakening and mind transforming devotional. Reading, meditating and applying the knowledge acquired from this book has been really rewarding. I really appreciate the fact that the author incorporates both biblical principles and experiential knowledge to support his perspective. This enables the content to be practical instead solely theoretical.

In addition, the daily journal challenges have helped me tremendously in my pursuit to allow the Word of God to guide my daily decisions and actions. Knowing and understanding God's Word is indeed the antidote to fear. This journey has been liberating. God bless you Mr. Morrison, and may the Holy Spirit continue to enlighten you about the character and principles of God.

Juanita Hutchinson-Blake
Educator

As I reflected on Day 4 of *Mind Renewal Devotional Volume* 1 titled "Celebrate Your Success," I realized that whenever I achieved something in life or something good happened to me, I tend to keep it on "a down low." My mentality has always been to give my best in whatever I set out to do. I will always go the extra mile or exert the extra effort in order to achieve whatever the intended goal may be. But I always hide my successes to prevent jealousy among my peers or making them feel less of themselves.

Fast forward, after indulging in the content of Day 4, I now understand that I should celebrate my hard work. I now respect my achievements in the past; as they too have led me to where I am today—stronger and wiser. I pledge to celebrate my successes as they are and were guided by God.

Justin Moses
Manager

To my father Wentworth Morrison.
Thank you for the wealth that you passed on to me. I appreciate your instructions and corrections.

INTRODUCTION

The mind is the factory where the decision of victory or defeat, poverty or wealth is conceived and pursued. It is easily the most valuable asset of one's possessions. One of the best gifts given to man by God is the ability to think. The dimension of one's thoughts is manifested daily through spoken words and deeds. This position is substantiated by Proverbs 23:7a, which reads, "As a man thinks in his heart so his hc."

Unfortunately, many minds are bankrupted with low level processing which produces unacceptable speech and actions. A depraved mind will serve as a barricade to new opportunities. There are possibilities that remain unknown because they reside outside of the parameters of healthy or renewed thinking.

This devotional series was birthed from the book, *Mind Renewal: Biblical Secrets to a Better You.* I truly believe that one of the greatest self-investment to be pursued is the renewing of your mind. This is volume two of a three-part series.

According to Romans 12:2, we should not conform to the world but rather be transformed by the renewing of our mind. The evidence of Mind Renewal will be heard and seen as daily transformation is pursued.

This 30-Day *Mind Renewal Transformation Devotional* serves as a vehicle to your transformation. This volume has five parts which cover topics: *It Starts with You; There is Great Wealth in Serving; Purpose-Driven Life; Scars* and *Next*.

Use it alongside the *Mind Renewal* book. This devotional is equipped with transforming stories, supporting scriptures, assignments and a daily journal page. The journal page is to be used to document your daily assignments, challenges and victories. I would advise you not to move on to another day before completing the assignments and journal of the present one.

Get ready to become a better you!

TABLE OF CONTENTS

PART 1: IT STARTS WITH YOU 1

    Day 1: Address Your Closet of Un-Pleasantries 1

    Day 2: Selective Grasp 5

    Day 3: Committed to Your Commitment 9

    Day 4: Practice Quick Forgiveness 12

    Day 5: Other's Faults Don't Make You an Angel ... 16

PART II: THERE IS GREAT WEALTH IN SERVING 19

    Day 6: Serving is Priceless 20

    Day 7: God Dictates, Not You 24

    Day 8: Clear Definitions 28

    Day 9: Invest in Others 32

    Day 10: Be a Blessing 36

    Day 11: Your Assignment is Your Key 40

    Day 12: Is Our Help Out of Self-Gain 44

PART III: PURPOSE DRIVEN LIFE 48

Day 13: There is Pain in the Will of God 49

Day 14: Weight of Purpose 53

Day 15: Rejecting the Easy Path 57

Day 16: Alignment with Purpose 62

Day 17: Am I Fulfilling My Purpose 66

Day 18: Blazing Trails 70

Day 19: Divine Closure 74

PART IV: SCARS 78

Day 20: Poverty 79

Day 21: Demonstrate Your Belief 83

Day 22: Shadow 87

Day 23: Ordered by God, Noy by Scars 91

Day 24: Let Criticism Work for You 95

Day 25: There is Room 99

Day 26: Chosen to Wear Your Scars 103

PART V: NEXT 107

Day 27: Letting Go What You Have Lost 108

Day 28: Greater Next, Greater Opposition 112

Day 29: Nothing Changes, Nothing New Experienced
.... 116

Day 30: Leave 121

CONCLUSION 125

ACKNOWLEDGEMENTS 125

ABOUT THE AUTHOR 128

PART 1:
IT STARTS WITH YOU

Day 1
ADDRESS YOUR CLOSET OF UN-PLEASANTRIES

Scripture Focus: John 12:5-7

To become a better you, you will have to address issues that have been hidden in your closet of un-pleasantries. These could be unresolved hurts, submission issues, envy in relationships, insecurities; love for malice, lying, being rebellious and you can add your individual truth to this list. Truth is, you can never pretend the pain away. That closed closet needs to be reopened and cleaned. Some need to be burned, killed and buried and others need to be addressed for mending.

Donnie McClurkin was not always the great Gospel artist he is today. He had some early un-pleasantries that he had to overcome. At eight (8) years old, he was raped by his uncle and at thirteen he was then raped by his uncle's son. At thirty-one he was diagnosed with Leukemia. McClurkin overcame traumatic events that would have destroyed his lesser man. He overcame, sexual abuse, family drug addiction, alcoholism and a life-threatening disease. He addressed his closet. He sought help from the church. The church sisters embarked on a journey of breaking his feminine tendencies.

Judas, one of Jesus' disciples had things in his closet that needed addressing. He failed to deal with his stealing tendencies. "Then saith one of his disciples, Judas Iscariot, Simon's son, which should betray him, why was not this ointment sold for three hundred pence, and given to the poor? This he said, not that he cared for the poor; but because he was a thief, and had the bag, and bare what was put therein" (John 12:5-7). This unaddressed un-pleasantry led to him betraying Jesus and committing suicide.

ASSIGNMENT

Make a list from your closet of un-pleasantries. Empty it. Convert that closet to a study.

Document your responses to the assignment as well as your challenges and victories.

_____

_____

_____

IT STARTS WITH YOU

MIND RENEWAL TRANSFORMATION DEVOTIONAL

Day 2
SELECTIVE GRASP

Scripture Focus: 2 Samuel 11:1-5

Ackaisha Green was inside the ATM at Central Police Station on East Queen Street in Downtown, Kingston when she stumbled upon a stash of cash suspected to be in the millions of dollars. She felt it was not hers to keep. The money could have gone a long way for the mother of two who ekes out a living in the InnerCity of James Street in Central Kingston. The Observer visited Green, and learned she received a heavy tongue-lashing from her mother who described her as "the stupidest of all my children." The mother said, "A mi she beg(she begged me) J$200 (US$1.50) this morning to give her son to go to school," the mother complained, with a loud hiss of her teeth. Green insisted that handing over the money was the right thing to do.

Unlike King David who saw that which was not his and coveted it, Green understood that the money did not belong to her and surrendered it to authorities. In 2 Samuel 11, we see the following:

> And David sent and enquired after the woman. And one said, Is not this Bathsheba, the daughter of Eliam, the wife of Uriah the Hittite? And David sent messengers and took her; and she came in unto him, and he lay with her; for she was purified from her uncleanness: and she returned unto her house." The account should have ended where David was told, she is the wife of Uriah. But he trampled the barriers of her marriage and slept with her."

As we renew our minds, let us come in agreement with this: *Not everything that is within our reach needs to be ours.* Touch not, taste not, and handle not that which is not yours. Ackaisha Green having done what is right, received $1.2 million in rewards among other gifts which celebrated her honesty

ASSIGNMENT

This might be challenging but return what you have in your possession that is not yours. Going forward, if it is not yours don't take it.

Document your responses to the assignment as well as your challenges and victories.

IT STARTS WITH YOU

MIND RENEWAL TRANSFORMATION DEVOTIONAL

Day 3
COMMITTED TO YOUR COMMITMENT

Scripture Focus: Genesis 6:13-22

Luther Younger walks six miles round-trip every day in the heat, rain and snow to visit Waverlee his wife in the hospital. Waverlee Younger was diagnosed with a brain tumor nearly nine years ago and doctors thought she'd have just five years to live. Lutheta, their daughter says both of her parents have remained extremely strong. Over the past nine years, Waverlee has been in and out of the hospital, sometimes for months at a time.

Luther stayed by her side, walking to the hospital to visit every day and often sleeping there, sometimes on the floor. Luther demonstrated being committed to his commitment. He committed himself to his wife and that did not cease because she became ill. Her illness excavated another level of his commitment. Any person who refuses to be committed to their commitment should not be trusted.

We are given an excellent example of being committed to your commitment from Noah in the book of Genesis. He received instructions from God to build an Ark in preparation for a flood that would destroy the world. As I researched, it is a popular belief that time frame it took for completion is 120 years. This is derived from Genesis 6:3, and the LORD said, "My Spirit shall not strive with man forever, for he is indeed flesh; yet his days shall be one hundred and twenty years." The time was long, but he was committed. Whatever you have committed yourself to, be it a marriage, job, team as long as it remains healthy, be committed to your commitment.

ASSIGNMENT

It might take a long time but complete your assignment. Note where you stopped or paused and restart

Document your responses to the assignment as well as your challenges and victories.

_____
_____
_____
_____
_____

IT STARTS WITH YOU

Day 4
PRACTICE QUICK FORGIVENESS

Scripture Focus: Matthew 6:14-15

The deaths of Peter Fleming, 27; Jim Elliot, 28; Ed McCully, 28; Roger Youderian, 31, and Nate Saint, 32, made headlines for weeks, and produced a bestseller. It was a best seller about the five missionaries who lost their lives in Ecuador. Fewer people know that their widows later led the killers and their tribe to the Christian faith and the tribe's conversion ended generations of tribal revenge killings.

In 1959, Nate Saint's sister Rachel and Jim Elliot's widow, Elisabeth, contacted the tribe. Rachel Saint remained with them for 30 years, and Steve Saint (Nate Saint's son) spent summers there from the age of nine. He was "adopted" by

Mincaye, the man who had killed his father. Steve said, once Mincaye scolded his aunt because Steve didn't know basic skills, such as how to make a blow gun. But "Aunt Rachel stuck her finger back at him and said, 'You, Mincaye, having killed his father -- who do you think should teach him how to live?" So Mincaye taught him how to live while his aunt taught Christianity

As I pursued becoming a better me, I came to terms with the importance of quick forgiveness. Quick forgiveness is rejecting the opportunity of festering ills and negative feelings. This truth was modelled by the missionaries to Ecuador. Members of the tribe killed Steve's father, but Steve Saint helped to change their society. After Rachel Saint's death in 1994, Mincaye asked him to help the tribe become less dependent on foreigners.

The Indigenous-People's Technology and Education Center founded by Mr. Saint now adapts dentistry and other skills for non-industrial cultures. Jesus was big on forgiveness, he said, "For if ye forgive men their trespasses, your heavenly Father will also forgive you, but if ye forgive not men their trespasses, neither will your Father forgive your trespasses.

ASSIGNMENT

Make a list of all those who you need to forgive. Start forgiving today!

MIND RENEWAL TRANSFORMATION DEVOTIONAL

Document your responses to the assignment as well as your challenges and victories.

_____
_____
_____
_____
_____
_____
_____
_____
_____
_____
_____
_____
_____
_____
_____
_____
_____
_____
_____
_____
_____
_____
_____

IT STARTS WITH YOU

Day 5
OTHER'S FAULTS DON'T MAKE YOU AN ANGEL

Scripture Focus: Matthew 7:1-5

My eldest brother once said, "he believes Judas was the best Christian." His reasoning was, Judas having recognized that he did something wrong against an innocent man, showed his remorse by killing himself. I don't believe he supports suicide but was making the point that he took responsibility for his wrongs. He was lamenting that persons are always blaming someone rather than admitting to their errors.

The failure to admit wrongs is a major contributor to the breakdown of many marriages. Two years into the marriage and now it's officially over! And the cry is, "If she was a better

IT STARTS WITH YOU

person, helped with the children, paid more attention, remembered our anniversary and my birth date, if only her family stayed out of our affairs, and only if she handled our finances better, then we would still be married." While all the above might be true, the harder and most important is, how did you contribute to the death of the marriage? The Bible is not silent on this. Mathew 7: 3-5 states:

> ...and why beholdest thou the mote that is in thy brother's eye, but considerest not the beam that is in thine own eye? Or how wilt thou say to thy brother, let me pull out the mote out of thine eye; and, behold, a beam is in thine own eye? Thou hypocrite, first cast out the beam out of thine own eye; and then shalt thou see clearly to cast out the mote out of thy brother's eye.

It's very easy to magnify the faults of others, while our own short comings are hidden. Your fault might not even be a deficiency because it looks good. But it's still a fault. In relationship counselling, a great question is: how did you contribute to where the marriage is right now?

ASSIGNMENT

Switch the focus to you. Fix you first! How do you plan to fix yourself first?

MIND RENEWAL TRANSFORMATION DEVOTIONAL

Document your responses to the assignment as well as your challenges and victories.

_____
_____
_____
_____
_____
_____
_____
_____
_____
_____
_____
_____
_____
_____
_____
_____
_____
_____
_____
_____

PART II:
THERE IS GREAT WEALTH IN SERVING

Day 6
SERVING IS PRICELESS

Scripture Focus: Matthew 20:20-28

In renewing our minds this is a position to embrace wholeheartedly —service to others is one of the highest achievements one can obtain. It was Nelson Mandela who said, "Real leaders must be ready to <u>sacrifice</u> all for the freedom of their people." As a good leader, you must get over self and learn the art of servitude. Jesus, the greatest leader of all times, according to Mathew 20:28 said, "I have not come to be served, but to serve." In proving his words to be true, he gave all —His life. John 3: 16 states, "for God so love the world, He gave His only begotten son, that whosoever believes on Him, will not perish but have eternal life."

greater *works* than these he will do, because I go to My Father" (John 14:12).

Jesus had the awesome opportunity of choosing his team (disciples) without the assistance of a board or a committee. Yet all His team forsook Him when He as he was led to fulfil His destiny of being crucified. Prominent among the team were Judas, who betrayed him, Peter who denied him and Thomas who doubted him. The truth is, if we were Jesus, we would not have chosen a team we knew would abandon us. But Jesus knew that, for His assignment to be fulfilled, He must serve those who would betray, deny, doubt and abandon him.

He was the leader, but not the only available vessel. He was not afraid to utilize the gifts and expertise of others. Judas was a thief who loved money. This truth was used in the accomplishment of Jesus's assignment. Some of the hardest to serve might just be your greatest assets to the fulfilment of your destiny. Serve with the big picture in mind, which is not you.

ASSIGNMENT

Serve someone who is not able to serve you in return.

Document your responses to the assignment as well as your challenges and victories.

_____

_____

_____

MIND RENEWAL TRANSFORMATION DEVOTIONAL

THERE IS GREAT WEALTH IN SERVING

Day 7
GOD DICTATES, NOT YOU

Scripture Focus: Acts 8:26-39

I heard a story of a pastor and his wife who had fallen on financial rough times. They prayed and asked God to send help, as nothing was in the house to eat. Part of the prayer was, "even a two footed John Crow." Shortly after prayer, a sister who had tried to do the wife harm, came bearing bags of groceries. Initially the wife rejected the food, but the pastor reminded her of their prayers.

Apostle Joshua Selman said, "God never trusts people He has not tested." One major test a person can receive from God is trusting Him to send the perfect help. You cannot dictate to God from where your help should come. We see in 1 Kings 17 God instructed a raven to feed His prophet Elijah at the brook Cherith during the time of drought. The raven brought him bread and flesh. And according to Luke

THERE IS GREAT WEALTH IN SERVING

16:201-21, a beggar laid at a rich man's gate desiring the crumbs that fell from his table.

The beggar was covered with sores. His help came from the lips of dogs, who licked his sores. The beggars' name was Lazarus. He was a human being, yet no help came from the human race. God showed us an example In Acts Chapter 8. A Eunuch was traveling and reading the holy scrolls, but he lacked understanding. God instructed Phillip to join himself to the Eunuch's company. The Eunuch was not travelling alone. Yet none of his companions was able to help.

Know this, God may send help from outside your circle. Phillip had understanding and imparted it to the Eunuch. He appreciated the help and desired baptism.

ASSIGNMENT

Repent of the many times you rejected help because it did not come in the package you expected. Prepare to receive from the Lord, the help He sends.

Document your responses to the assignment as well as your challenges and victories.

_____
_____
_____
_____

MIND RENEWAL TRANSFORMATION DEVOTIONAL

THERE IS GREAT WEALTH IN SERVING

Day 8
CLEAR DEFINITIONS

Scripture Focus: Matthew 13:21

No one enjoys failing. Yet many have and will fail because they did not master the process of effectively changing roles as life requires. This is recipe for segmental failures. Jesus knew how to navigate between roles and did so effectively. Some saw him as the Messiah. "The next day John saw Jesus coming toward him and said, "Look, the Lamb of God, who takes away the sin of the world!" (John 1:29). Some saw Him as the great healer. "When Jesus had entered Capernaum, a centurion came to him, asking for help. "Lord," he said, "my servant lies at home paralyzed, suffering terribly." Jesus said to him, "I shall come and heal him?" The centurion replied, "Lord, I do not deserve to have you come under my roof. But just say the word, and my servant will be healed"(- Mathew 8: 5-8).

Others knew Him as the food provider. "We have here only five loaves of bread and two fish," they answered. "Bring them here to me," he said. And he directed the people to sit down on the grass. Taking the five loaves and the two fish and looking up to heaven, he gave thanks and broke the loaves. Then he gave them to the disciples, and the disciples gave them to the people" (Matthew 14:17). They all ate and were satisfied, and the disciples picked up twelve baskets full of broken pieces that were left over.

Some years ago, I listened Joyce Meyer as she spoke about her different roles. When she is at work, she is the boss and the pastor. At home she must take off the hat of lead role and submit to her husband. To the congregation she is Pastor but to her husband, she is his submitted wife. Truth is, you're not the same to everyone.

ASSIGNMENT

Be intentional in deciphering what's your role to the persons you meet. Act accordingly. Make a list of where you have been forced into roles. Then pursue if warranted, override the verdict handed to you.

Document your responses to the assignment as well as your challenges and victories.

_____

_____

THERE IS GREAT WEALTH IN SERVING

MIND RENEWAL TRANSFORMATION DEVOTIONAL

Day 9
INVEST IN OTHERS

Scripture Focus: Luke 10:25-37

I love the account of the Good Samaritan found in Luke 10: 30-35. A Jewish man was travelling and was robbed by thieves, beaten stripped and left to die. Two temple officials, namely a Levite and a Priest passed him without rendering any assistance.

A Samaritan whom the Jews had no dealings with, saw him and assisted him. He set him on his mule and walked; took him to an inn, paid for treatment and stayed. Afterwards he left him and told the inn keeper to take care of him, and upon return, if the Jewish man incurred an additional expense, he would pay.

He taught us this truth —*You don't need reasons to invest in God's people.* Do it and expect nothing in return. When you give to others, you are lending to God (Prov.19:17). One act of godly investment can change the course of generations.

Mrs. Alrick Trewick and her husband, the late Dr. Trewick, invested in my mother and her five children. From sending monthly Reader's Digest to promote reading, pre-paid high school cafeteria lunch monies, to assistance with Seminary tuition fees.

They invested without being asked. In return, Mrs Trewick asked that each child finds someone and contribute to the uplifting of that person and keep the cycle going. The cycle of investing in others is so powerful, it shifts you from being selfish. Investment without the expectations of return to yourself, makes giving light.

ASSIGNMENT

Invest in someone's future who is not your child or your parents. How will you invest?

Document your responses to the assignment as well as your challenges and victories.

_____

_____

_____

_____

_____

MIND RENEWAL TRANSFORMATION DEVOTIONAL

THERE IS GREAT WEALTH IN SERVING

Day 10
BE A BLESSING

Scripture: 2 Kings 5:1-14

14-year-old Archie Williams was sentenced to life in prison without parole in 1983, for a rape and stabbing of a woman in East Baton Rouge Parish. But after 36 years of incarceration, he was vindicated. The 19th Judicial District Court of East Baton Rouge, Louisiana's ruling was based on new evidence of Williams's innocence. There was a search in the FBI's national fingerprint database which linked fingerprints left at the crime scene to the true assailant. This man committed at least five other rapes in the years after the 1982 rape, for which Williams was wrongly convicted.

When asked how he felt about finally being released from prison for a crime he did not commit, Williams reflected and responded. "There are many innocent people at Angola, guys who have served over 50 years. **I'm happy to be cleared finally, but I'm not free until they are free.**" Mr. Williams wants to help other inmates who are innocent to be vindicated.

In 2 Kings Chapter 5, we learn about a slave girl, who despite being taken into captivity away from her hometown, shared love with the one who enslaved her. She told Naaman, her captor, about Elisha the prophet, who was able to make him whole from his leprosy. She demonstrated the power of not allowing the wrongs done to her, to block her from being a blessing to someone. Like Archie Williams, she wanted the best for those with whom she shared time and space. Although hurt, she gave love.

ASSIGNMENT

Love on someone who have done you wrong. Be intentional about it. Who will be the recipient?

Document your responses to the assignment as well as your challenges and victories.

_____
_____
_____

THERE IS GREAT WEALTH IN SERVING

MIND RENEWAL TRANSFORMATION DEVOTIONAL

Day 11
YOUR ASSIGNMENT IS YOUR KEY

Scripture Focus: 1 Samuel 16: 17-23, 17: 17-22

A few years ago, I received a prophetic word that God is changing my assignment. Shortly, after I applied for a job. I was interviewed and contacted some days later and was advised that I was selected for the position. However, I would be contacted after the offer was finalized.

Weeks and months went by and I received no further correspondence. During my waiting period, the church I attended had a function and I volunteered to serve as a waiter. It was fun serving. During serving, a church sister called and introduced me to a minister of Government. It so happened that the minister oversaw the Department to which I had applied. The minister commented on my service.

He said I was observed, and I saw that you served with joy. I relayed my situation and the government minister promised to investigate it. I was also given the minister's personal number and told to call the following Monday as a reminder. This I did and I started working after the minister got things rolling. Interestingly, the job for which I applied was not the one I got. The one I got was in alignment with my new assignment.

Jesse's son David was trained and prepared by God to be a deliverer for Israel. Yet we see him, never forcing himself into the position. He was sent by his father to the battle ground and he was beckoned by King Saul. I have come to accept this, if God gave you the assignment, you don't have to force your way in, and the door will be opened unto you at the right time. The God who sent you on the assignment will cause the eyes of those in authority to take notice of you. There is no need to bribe, lie or fight against someone who is already in proximity.

ASSIGNMENT

Make a note of two assignments you forced yourself into. Record the outcome. Next assignment, allow God to do it.

Document your responses to the assignment as well as your challenges and victories.

_____

_____

_____

MIND RENEWAL TRANSFORMATION DEVOTIONAL

THERE IS GREAT WEALTH IN SERVING

Day 12
IS OUR HELP GIVEN OUT OF SELF-GAIN?

Scripture Focus: Exodus 2:11-15

The hidden wealth of acting outside of the parameters of benefitting self is a treasure that needs to be excavated with all urgency. The truth is, behind the veil of personal acquisition, the expanse of serving a community or a nation, resides the joy of serving others, waiting to be captured. Unfortunately, we are so buried head deep into self that we are blinded to the magnificent wealth that is untouched.

In Exodus 2, we see Moses assisting a slave who was being mistreated. Moses aided without expecting anything in return. And even though this led to him having to flee from his home, it was worth it. It was after his selfless act, he learned shepherding, got a wife, two sons and had his first miraculous encounter with Jehovah. In this encounter, he received his life's assignment. Which was to go and deliver the children of Israel and take them to the Promise Land. Truth is many persons live and die without ever discovering what their life's assignment is. But not Moses. It can easily be said, the selfless act of helping the mistreated slave, served as the key to unlocking his future. What will your selfless future unlocking key be and will you activate it? It might not be the first or tenth act, but keeping doing good. Not waiting for that unlocking but for the joy of helping

ASSIGNMENT

A) When was the last time you did a selfless act, expecting nothing in return?

B) Record your next three selfless acts and how you felt after doing each

Document your responses to the assignment as well as your challenges and victories.

_____
_____
_____
_____
_____

THERE IS GREAT WEALTH IN SERVING

MIND RENEWAL TRANSFORMATION DEVOTIONAL

PART III:
PURPOSE- DRIVEN LIFE

Day 13
THERE IS PAIN IN THE WILL OF GOD

Scripture Focus: Luke 22:40-44

I remember being invited to speak at a church and as I sought the Lord for the message, I heard in my Spirit, "There is pain in the will of God." Renew your mind with this: there is purpose in your pain. Your purpose will not be realized without your all. You will find your purpose in the will of God.

Pastor David Grant worked as a manager at a construction company. The Lord told him to resign and do ministry full time. He was the sole monetary earner of six. He obeyed and things got very tight financially. One Sunday, he spoke at a function and received a honorary gift. It was a welcome gift as he had no money for the four children to go to school the following morning. Then he heard the Holy Spirit said, "Sow it back into the ministry." It was painful but he did it. He understood that the will of God must supersede the pain he felt. Before he left the venue, a sister said the Lord told her to bless him financially. It was a good size blessing.

Jesus is our primary example. He experienced choosing the pain in the will of God over His will. In Luke 22: 42 he said, "Father, if thou be willing, remove this cup from me: nevertheless, not my will, but thine, be done." Jesus knew what awaited Him. Judas's betrayal, arrest, denial by Peter, and abandoned by all his disciples. He would be lied on, scourged, spat on and crucified.

The magnitude of the pain caused him to pray in such agony, his sweat became like drops of blood. Yet he sounded the alarm, not my will but yours be done Father. In other words, He declared his complete commitment to the will of God. Will you embrace the pain associated with the will of God? He pursued the will of God through the pain and completed the redemption package. Salvation is now free because of His sacrifice.

ASSIGNMENT

Do a personal evaluation of your level of commitment to God. How have you responded to the pain associated with the will of God?

MIND RENEWAL TRANSFORMATION DEVOTIONAL

Document your responses to the assignment as well as your challenges and victories.

_____
_____
_____
_____
_____
_____
_____
_____
_____
_____
_____
_____
_____
_____
_____
_____
_____
_____
_____
_____
_____

PURPOSE DRIVEN LIFE

Day 14
WEIGHT OF PURPOSE

Scripture Focus: Numbers 20: 10-11

All divine purpose received from the Lord, comes with associated weight. Truth is, the burden of your purpose has the potential to cause you to abort it. The longer the weight is carried, the more likely it is to cause additional pain. From the book, "Getting Back to Happy" we see the following.

Twenty years ago, when Angel and I were just undergrads in college, our psychology professor taught us a lesson we've never forgotten. On the last day of class before graduation, she walked up on stage to teach one final lesson, which she called "a vital lesson on the power of perspective and mindset." As she raised a glass of water over her head, everyone expected her to mention the typical "glass half empty or glass half full" metaphor. Instead, with a smile on her face, our professor asked, "How heavy is this glass of water I'm holding?" Students shouted out answers ranging from a couple of ounces to a couple of pounds. After a few moments of fielding answers and nodding her head, she replied, "From my perspective, the absolute weight of this glass is irrelevant. It all depends on how long I hold it. If I hold it for a minute or two, it's light. If I hold it for an hour straight, its weight might make my arm ache. If I hold it for a day straight, my arm will likely cramp up and feel completely numb and paralyzed, forcing me to drop the glass to the floor. In each case, the absolute weight of the glass doesn't change, but the longer I hold it, the heavier it feels to me."

Moses, the designated deliverer and leader of the children of Israel, was burdened down from the weight of his purpose. The people complained against Moses because of thirst. God spoke to him saying, he should speak to the rock for water to come forth. However according to Numbers 20: 10-11:

> And Moses and Aaron gathered the congregation together before the rock, and he said unto them, Hear now, ye rebels; must we fetch you water out of this rock? And Moses lifted his hand, and with his rod he smote the rock twice: and the water came out abundantly, and the congregation drank, and their beasts also.

Moses was angry at the Rebels. This caused him to disobey God's instructions. This saw him not entering the Promise Land.

ASSIGNMENT

What is the weight of your assignment? Develop coping mechanisms

Document your responses to the assignment as well as your challenges and victories.

PURPOSE DRIVEN LIFE

Day 15
REJECTING THE EASY PATH

Scripture Focus: Matthew 16: 21-25

Joseph was experiencing employment famine, but he continued to search. He tried the Classifieds in all the prominent newspapers, but to no avail. He visited his uncle and after hearing his plight, he offered Joseph a trip to England. Joseph was ecstatic but it was short lived. The trip meant Joseph transporting illegal substances. He needed the money, but the easy path could also mean incarceration. Joseph opted to continue searching the Classifieds.

Jesus demonstrated this truth according to Mathew 16: 21-23:

> From that time forth began Jesus to shew unto his disciples, how that he must go unto Jerusalem, and suffer many things of the elders and chief priests

and scribes, and be killed, and be raised again the third day. The Peter took him and began to rebuke him saying, be it far from thee Lord; this shall not be unto thee. [23]But he turned, and said unto Peter, Get thee behind me, Satan: thou art an offence unto me: for thou savourest not the things that be of God, but those that be of men.

Jesus rejected Peter's words which went against his destiny. You must not allow the easy path to rob you of fulfilling your purpose. Stay your course and say "Oh Lord, help me to accept my destiny and not divert from the path.

When the soldiers came to arrest Jesus, He said to His disciples who wanted to fight. "Thinkest thou that I cannot now pray to my father and shall presently give me more than twelve legions of angels? But how then will the Scriptures be fulfilled?" Jesus had an easy path out, but He pursued His purpose. Truth is, sometimes it's very challenging to not accept the easy path. But let us consider carefully what we have to lose.

ASSIGNMENT

While the easy is more attractive, the path chosen for you is the best. Reject the easy for the best. List two easy things that need rejecting.

Document your responses to the assignment as well as your challenges and victories.

PURPOSE-DRIVEN LIFE

MIND RENEWAL TRANSFORMATION DEVOTIONAL

PURPOSE-DRIVEN LIFE

Day 16
ALIGNMENT WITH PURPOSE

Scripture Focus: Luke 2:25-38

Your failure or victory is critical to the outcome of the lives of others. Today, we enjoy the convenience of the light bulb. We no longer have to fill our lamps with oil. We get light by the flip of a switch. As an inventor, Edison made 1,000 unsuccessful attempts at inventing the light bulb. When a reporter asked, "How did it feel to fail 1,000 times?" Edison replied, "I didn't fail 1,000 times. The light bulb was an invention with 1,000 steps."[1] He pursued his purpose and today we reap the fruits of his labour.

---

[1] https://www.uky.edu/~eushe2/Pajares/OnFailingG.html.

Rev. David Grant was sent to pastor a church in Morant Bay, St. Thomas, Jamaica in 2007. The church was in a terrible state reducing from more than (300 to seventeen 17 members, which included nine (9) children. A few weeks after he commenced his new assignment, a lady from the community approached him and said; "I have been waiting for you. The Lord showed me in a dream, you coming to pastor the church. Now I will attend." The lady believed that God had spoken to her, and she waited for the fulfilment. This was the first church Rev. Grant pastored.

We remember Simeon in the book of Luke. He was told by the Holy Spirit that he would not die before he saw the Messiah. After the birth of Jesus, His parents took Him to the temple to be blessed. Simeon upon seeing the child, took him up in his arms, blessed God, and said,

"Lord, now lettest thou thy servant depart in peace, according to thy word: For mine eyes have seen thy salvation." Simeon saw what he was waiting for. That which he was promised, was fulfilled. He confidently rejoiced in requesting to be taken home to glory.

ASSIGNMENT

Change your attitude towards your assignments. Lives are waiting on you.

Document your responses to the assignment as well as your challenges and victories.

MIND RENEWAL TRANSFORMATION DEVOTIONAL

PURPOSE DRIVEN LIFE

Day 17
AM I FULFILLING MY PURPOSE?

Scripture Focus: Exodus 3: 10, Joshua 1:2

One of the most frequently asked question is, "Am I fulfilling my purpose?" In the not too far distance you will hear, "What is my purpose?" Let us look at the life of Moses. Did Moses fulfill or failed to accomplish his purpose as instructed by God? Numbers chapter 20: 12 reads, "And the LORD spake unto Moses and Aaron, because ye believed me not, to sanctify me in the eyes of the children of Israel, therefore ye shall not bring this congregation into the land which I have given them."

This statement sounds damning and can easily be interpreted as a rebuke to one who failed to complete his purpose. However, let's look at Exodus 3:10, "God says to Moses, "Come now therefore, and I will send thee unto Pharaoh, that thou mayest bring forth my people the children of Israel out of Egypt." That was Moses' assignment. His purpose was never stated to bring them into the land of promise. Based on Exodus 3:10, he would have completed his purpose

However, his predecessor, Joshua had a different mandate. Let's examine. Joshua 1:2, "Moses my servant is dead; now therefore arise, go over this Jordan, thou, and all this people, unto the land which I do give to them, even to the children of Israel." Joshua's purpose was clearly different from Moses'. The people had already left Egypt, his task was to take them into the Promise Land. Both Moses and his servant Joshua fulfilled their purposes.

From the Scriptures shared, we see both men knowing their purposes from God. God is your Creator, the orchestrator of your best life. Therefore, He knows what are his plans towards you as stated in Jeremiah 29:11. We come into knowledge of our purpose from God our father.

ASSIGNMENT

Spend some time seeking God for knowledge of your purpose. Then pursue in obedience.

Document your responses to the assignment as well as your challenges and victories.

_____

_____

_____

MIND RENEWAL TRANSFORMATION DEVOTIONAL

THE PURPOSE-DRIVEN LIVE

Day 18
BLAZING TRAILS

Scripture Focus: John 1: 26-36

Andrew was raised in a single parent home, headed by his mother. He never knew his father. He had no father role model; no example to follow. When Andrew began fatherhood, he purposed in his heart to be the best Dad there was. His first child was his stepson. He loved that boy as though he was his biological child. He then got two children of his own

He gave them everything he didn't get. He had no trail to pattern, but he blazed an excellent one. He ensured that his children had a great example to follow. Andrew proved that the trail you blaze can become the pursued example. Before his children were conceived, the trail was already being prepared for them. He knew he was their forerunner, even though he had none

Like Jesus, before He was conceived, His Destiny Helper was already decided. John the Baptist, Jesus' cousin was the forerunner to Jesus. God positioned John to announce Jesus as the Messiah. When questioned, John declared, "I *am* the voice of one crying in the wilderness, make straight the way of the Lord, as said the Prophet Esaias." Then when Jesus showed up, John said, "Behold the Lamb of God, which taketh away the sin of the world. This is he of whom I said, after me cometh a man which is preferred before me: for he was before me."

Be cognizant of this truth, some trail is prepared for you, and others you will have to blaze. Jesus himself had to blaze the trail of salvation through death and resurrection. This was no easy task. The strain of it was increased especially since there will never be another to walk this journey. This was a one-time trail. Jesus came through a one-time trail –the virgin birth and was required to blaze a one-time trail -death for all sin.

ASSIGNMENT

Which trail are you commissioned to tread or blaze?

Document your responses to the assignment as well as your challenges and victories.

MIND RENEWAL TRANSFORMATION DEVOTIONAL

PURPOSE DRIVEN LIFE

Day 19
DIVINE CLOSURE

Scripture Focus: John 8: 1-11

Some years ago, Maxine received a late-night telephone call. The male on the other end said, "God says don't do it." She said she was preparing to have sexual intimacy with a friend who was at her home. She was disappointed but the fear of God prevented her from pursuing the act. That door of intimacy was closed.

About three years later, she told the gentleman that called that she recently found out that the guy she was about to have sex with that night was HIV positive. Maxine rejoiced at the divine closure she was granted. She is now married and recently gave birth to her third child.

As you renew your minds, always remember, the closed doors you are wailing about now and trying to reopen, were divinely shut to prevent you from aborting your purpose. In

John Chapter 8, we read the account of a woman caught in adultery and brought to Jesus. By the standard of the law, both she and the male should be put to death.

However, she was brought alone. Jesus told the accusing crowd, "Ye without sin cast the first stone" They all dropped their stones and walked away. But Jesus said something very powerful to her. He said, "your sins have been forgiven, go your way and sin no more." In other words, I have divinely closed the door of your deserving death but now you need to close the door to sin.

ASSIGNMENT

Stop crying over the doors that have been closed unto you. Start rejoicing, look forward to the new. What doors have been closed to you?

Document your responses to the assignment as well as your challenges and victories.

_____
_____
_____
_____
_____
_____
_____

MIND RENEWAL TRANSFORMATION DEVOTIONAL

PART IV: SCARS

Day 20
POVERTY

Scripture: 2 Kings 4: 1-7

A dear friend of many years, cried unto the Lord saying: "Lord I have been faithful to you. I have not desecrated my body. I pay my tithes faithfully. I serve in the church above the call of and I work hard. Therefore God, why do I have it so hard financially? I know I am not the worst and I'm not lazy."

She said the Lord responded to her with these words, "What happened to the songs?" The Holy Spirit had downloaded to her several songs. He also blessed her with a beautiful singing voice and the anointing to minister. She sang on her church choir when she lived in Jamaica and sings on her church choir in the USA. Basically, God pushed it back on her.

She was experiencing poverty not because God had abandoned her, but because she had failed to convert the resources given to her into meaningful means. She was responsible for her lack or her abundance. In 2017, she commenced voice training classes on the premise that she wanted to give God her best. To date, she is yet to record one song. She has not utilized what she has been given to eliminate her poverty.

The Prophet Elisha in 2 Kings 4, asked the widow woman what she had in her house. She responded, "only a jar of oil," after lamenting about the death of her husband and the debts he left her. The creditors were coming to take her sons as payment. Elijah needed something to work with. She had a jar of oil. What you have might look insignificant, but it is more than enough for God to use. Elijah. He told her to gather all the empty containers she could and fill them with oil. By faith she poured until all her jars were filled. She had enough to pay off her debts and to live off the rest. She moved from being in debt to debt free.

ASSIGNMENT

What is it you have? Time for conversion. Begin the process of converting it into meaningful means.

Document your responses to the assignment as well as your challenges and victories.

MIND RENEWAL TRANSFORMATION DEVOTIONAL

SCARS

Day 21
DEMONSTRATE YOUR BELIEF

Scripture: Matthew 17:22-23; 28: 5-9

In John chapter 20, there is an account of Thomas doubting the resurrection of Jesus. When Jesus saw Thomas, He told him to touch his scars, which stood as testimony of his death and resurrection. Thomas then believed. Thomas was transformed mentally and spiritually upon having a physical exposure to Jesus's scars. Your scars are powerful, stop being ashamed of them.

International Speaker, Joyce Meyer said she had been raped more than 200 times and that her father abused her at least once a week. She said he also abused her classmates and neighbors as well. She was forced to look at pornography.

She said: He didn't force me physically, but through lies, manipulation, fears and threats. I was sexually, mentally, emotionally and verbally abused by my father as far back as I can remember, until I finally left home at age 18.

She told her audience God can help them through even the most challenging times After opening up about her personal experience, Meyer emphasized that people can trust God to transform their lives. She hopes that her transparency enables other people suffering abuse to seek help, knowing healing from abuse is possible through God. The abuse she endured were not physical scars that are easily seen, but emotional and mental.

Stop being ashamed of your scars, they tell your story. Wear your scars proudly. They testify loudly that, you are not a quitter, you went through the fire and the flood and made it. You did not give in to the urge to commit suicide. You are more than conquers. Like Joyce Meyer, your scars have the potential to be a source of encouragement and healing. Someone is waiting to hear your story.

ASSIGNMENT

Stop being ashamed of your scars. Use them to help someone. You might not have the platform like Joyce Meyer, but that individual you know is hurting, please help.

PURPOSE-DRIVEN LIFE

Document your responses to the assignment as well as your challenges and victories.

MIND RENEWAL TRANSFORMATION DEVOTIONAL

Day 22
SHADOW

Scripture Focus: Genesis 29: 15-32

Often, we hear and see the generation before trying to live their best lives through the generation that follows. Children are handcuffed to the ideals of their parents and get lost in discovering their parents' strength and weaknesses. My best friend from High School was pressured into Teacher's college. This was his mom's desire. He pursued and graduated but spent about one semester teaching. This was not what he wanted.

Many persons die without knowing and fulfilling their divine purpose because they choose to live in another's shadow. You must ask the difficult question: *Whose life are you living? Yours, your family or friends?* The pursuit of happiness through the shadow of another will result in self-destruction. Don't deprive the world of knowing your uniqueness. This includes your scars. They distinguish and separate you, therefore embrace them.

In the book of Genesis chapter 29, Jacob worked for Rachel but was tricked into marrying Leah. Leah's father thought it not wise to give the younger daughter before the older one. Leah suffered because of his decision. Verse 31 reads:

> .and when the LORD saw that Leah was hated, he opened her womb: but Rachel was barren. And Leah conceived, and bare a son, and she called his name Reuben: for she said, surely the LORD hath looked upon my affliction; now therefore my husband will love me.

She was hated and desired the love of her husband. Her father pushed her to live in the shadow of her sister Rachel. But she never measured up to Rachel in the eyes of Jacob.

ASSIGNMENT

This might be challenging to admit, but look diligently, are you living in someone's shadow? Remove and pursue your own life.

Document your responses to the assignment as well as your challenges and victories.

SCARS

MIND RENEWAL TRANSFORMATION DEVOTIONAL

Day 23

ORDERED BY GOD, NOT BY SCARS

Scripture Focus: Psalms 37:23

One truth you should never lose grip of is: *your steps are ordered by God, not by the events of your past/scars.* According to an article on the Muse Stephen King never gave up.

Stephen King was broke and struggling when he was first trying to write. He and his wife were so poor they had to borrow clothes for their wedding and had gotten rid of the telephone because it was too expensive. King received so many rejection letters for his works that he developed a system for collecting them. He received 60 rejections before selling his first short story, "The Glass Floor," for $35. Even his now best-selling book, Carrie, wasn't a hit at first. After dozens of rejections, he finally sold it for a meager advance to Doubleday Publishing, where the hardback sold only 13,000 copies—not great. Soon after, though, Signet Books signed on for the paperback rights for $400,000, $200,000 of which went to King. Success achieved![2]

For King his past was riddled with rejection, poverty and hard work. Yours might be abortion, murder, stealing, and incarceration etc. Whatever your scars of the past are, please understand that the enemy will try to use them against you. However, you can convert that mess into your message. The Bible tells us in Psalm 37:23, "The steps of a good man are ordered by the LORD: and he delighteth in his way." Rejection might just be the push you need to succeed.

ASSIGNMENT

It's time to revisit some goals you gave up on. Their realities are still possible. Pursue.

Document your responses to the assignment as well as your challenges and victories.

_____

_____

---

[2] https://www.themuse.com/advice/9-famous-people-who-will-inspire-you-to-never-give-up,

SCARS

MIND RENEWAL TRANSFORMATION DEVOTIONAL

Day 24
LET YOUR SCARS

Scripture Focus: Provers 12:17

The error of undervaluing your scars is a crime that unfortunately continues to be committed. When I wrote my first book, *Mind Renewal: Biblical Secrets to a Better You*, it was challenging but inspiring. I felt awesome having submitted the manuscript to the editor. The process was explained, and I anticipated the rewrite.

What I was not prepared for were some of the comments from my editor. Words like, *awkward, consider removing, and doesn't fit*. Somehow, the first of these, struck like swords. I had to quickly embrace the wealth of her criticism. As I rewrote sections, based on her critique, I started rejoicing knowing that my editor knows what she is doing. She made sense. Her critique highlighted the scar of rejection that I had skillfully hidden but not addressed. Rejection was a sore enemy of mine until I recognize that my enemy is sometimes my best friend. For years I missed out on the wealth of rejection. The book was better because she critiqued it truthfully.

As you renew your mind, take the intended negative battering of your scars and convert it to your prosperity. Rather than seeing scars as shameful, something to be hidden, please begin to reap. You might say, "it depends on who is criticizing." Is it the intent to expose your scars to belittle or is it to improve your progress? Do they have your best interest at heart? Whatever the intent, use them as guides to transform your life and move forward.

The truth sometimes hurts, but it's better than soothing lies. Let us embrace this wealth key: *Your scars are your wealth.* See your scars as more valuable than money. One scar converted to an asset can positively influence millions. Let your scars work for you

ASSIGNMENT

As of today, never frown on any of your scars. Instead, extract the wealth embedded in them. How will you extract their wealth?

Document your responses to the assignment as well as your challenges and victories.

SCARS

MIND RENEWAL TRANSFORMATION DEVOTIONAL

Day 25
THERE IS ROOM

Scripture Focus: Philippians 3:7-14

Recently, I sat down to watch a movie. A private contractor had the responsibility of checking if prisoners were able to escape. To do this, they sent in a specialist posing as an inmate. His job was to escape. After escaping, they met with the operators of the prison, critiqued their operations and exposed their weaknesses. The operators must now improve their facilities and services. The operators knew they had not maximized their security and pursued to achieve greater security.

One lecturer reportedly said, I never give a 100 % grade. There is always room for improvement. I truly believe as long as life permits, there will be room for self-improvement. You will never attain the status of "no room for self –improvement." Your scar is one tool, if employed properly, that can aid this process of self-improvement. Scars and weaknesses show that you are human. Rather than caving under the weight of the exposure of our shortcomings, let us strive to improve our weak areas without beating down ourselves.

The well-learned Paul, the Apostle said, "Brethren, I count not myself to have apprehended: but this one thing I do, forgetting those things which are behind, and reaching forth unto those things which are before, I press toward the mark for the prize of the high calling of God in Christ Jesus" (Philippians 3:13-14). Paul made it abundantly clear, that he had not achieved it all. There was more for him to improve. This is a great Mind Renewal key. Keep pressing upward!

ASSIGNMENT

Make a list of three areas that need improvement. Start working on the easiest, then graduate to the hardest. It might be your relationship with God. Spend more time together.

Document your responses to the assignment as well as your challenges and victories.

_____

_____

_____

SCARS

MIND RENEWAL TRANSFORMATION DEVOTIONAL

Day 26
CHOSEN TO WEAR YOUR SCARS

Scripture Focus: 2 Corinthians 12:7-10

Your scars validate who you say you are. Kahlil Gibran author of *The Prophet posits*, said "Out of suffering have emerged the strongest souls; the most massive characters are seared with scars." You see your scars as disabilities but let them become your platform of motivation. You can find your purpose out of your pain, ridicule and indifference.

Like Nick Vujicic who had to learn this hard truth, and he did. At birth, his mother refused to hold him, but she then understood that God choose this path for him. The following is an excerpt from his story.[3]

> Nick Vujicic is 33 years old. He was born with an extremely rare congenital disorder known as Phocomelia, which is characterized by the absence of legs and arms. Growing up in Melbourne, Australia, Nick struggled mentally, emotionally, and physically. Bullied at school, he attempted suicide when he was just 10 years old. Eventually coming to terms with his disability, Nick decided to become vocal about living with disabilities and finding hope and meaning in life. The charismatic Australian now travels the world addressing huge crowds. He has visited more than 57 countries and given over three thousand talks, some of which have attracted audiences as large as 110,000 people. He has also published his memoir Love Without Limits, is married and father of two sons.

Paul the Apostle sought God in 2 Corinthians 12 for relieve from a condition but it was not granted. He concludes that he takes pleasure in his infirmity. Instead of wasting time trying to fit in and resemble the society's dictates and norms, pursue a degree in accepting who you are and finding your life's purpose and destiny.

---

[3] https://yourstory.com/2016/05/nick-vujicic/

ASSIGNMENT

Use your infirmities and scars to propel you into being your best you. Mentor someone. Help them to change their life.

Document your responses to the assignment as well as your challenges and victories.

SCARS

PART V: NEXT

Day 27
LETTING GO WHAT YOU HAVE LOST

Scripture Focus: Genesis 12

Here lies your deliverance: *your best days are still to be lived.* Yesterday was good. Today is great but tomorrow shall be your greatest. In Genesis chapter 12, God spoke to Abram and told him to leave his family, his country and go to a land he knew not. He was challenged by God to lose that which he knew for that which was promised. Many persons have terminated their journey at this crossroads because of the fear of letting go the past for the future. The past is known but the future a mystery. However, you will never receive what is in store for you until you let go what you have lost.

Author Rose Costas said:

> It took me a long time to recognize that every day is a gift. I spent my entire life being angry and bitter with my parents for abandoning me as a child. I wanted them to suffer for leaving me behind but, unfortunately, the person who was suffering most was me. I lacked self-esteem and confidence. I couldn't trust anyone, and I lived in fear of ever forming an intimate bond with anyone for the fear they would leave me as well. I held myself hostage because I refuse to forgive them and to move on. I couldn't see that there wasn't anything I could do or say that could change what happened to me. I couldn't go back and change the past, even though, I wish I could many times. I had to accept that, that was the card I was dealt.

Rose Costas came to realize that she was the one holding herself in bondage. She lost precious years with her parents. But to get what is in store for her now, she must let go off the hurts.

ASSIGNMENT

Don't deprive yourself of your best by living in yesterday. It is time to emotionally spring clean. Lose the attachments that have strapped you to yesterday. Put on new shoes for tomorrow.

NEXT

Document your responses to the assignment as well as your challenges and victories.

MIND RENEWAL TRANSFORMATION DEVOTIONAL

Day 28
GREATER NEXT, GREATER OPPOSITION

Scripture Focus: Genesis 37, 39-41

We all get hit by unforeseen obstacles. For Kriss Carr, it was a rare cancer. On February 14, 2003, Carr was diagnosed with a rare Stage IV cancer called *epithelioid hemangioendothelioma* affecting her liver and her lungs. Carr fought her disease head on with a new nutritional lifestyle, developing a career as a successful author and health coach in the process.

Despite facing challenging circumstances from the start, she is now seen as one of the most knowledgeable experts on healthy living online today. She is the author of books like: *Crazy Sexy Diet: Eat Your Veggies, Ignite Your Spark, and Live Like You Mean It!* Carr's Great Next came by way of the big opposition of sickness. Unlike many persons, she used her opposition to propel her Next.

Without knowing, Joseph's brother's hatred for him catapulted him into his great Next. In Genesis 37, we read the account of Joseph and his brothers' hatred for him. Their hatred stemmed from their father's love for him (he loved him more than the others) and his dreams of reigning over them.

One day Joseph's father sent him to check on his brothers as they tended to their father's flock. They decided to kill him. They aborted that plan and threw him into a pit but then sold him into slavery. He was further sold to Potiphar, an Egyptian, who was captain of the guards of Pharaoh. Joseph served well but his master's wife pursued him.

He rejected her and she lied on him. He was imprisoned because of this lie. One night, Pharaoh had two dreams and only Joseph was able to interpret them. Pharaoh then promoted Joseph to be the second in command over all of Egypt. Joseph's Great Next was ushered in by great opposition.

ASSIGNMENT

Make a list of three great opposition. Now refocus your thinking, see the Great Next.

Document your responses to the assignment as well as your challenges and victories.

NEXT

MIND RENEWAL TRANSFORMATION DEVOTIONAL

Day 29
NOTHING CHANGES NOTHING NEW EXPERIENCED

Scripture Focus: Acts 16:16-34

In 1993, Mary's 20-year-old son got into a scuffle with 16-year-old Oshea Israel. Oshea killed Mary's son and spent 17 years in prison paying the price for what he did as a teen. Mary was furious; she believed Oshea was an "animal" and "deserved to be caged." Years after the sentencing, she visited him in prison.

"I wanted to know if you were in the same mindset of what I remembered from court, where I wanted to go over and hurt you," said Johnson to Israel. "But you were not that 16-year-old. You were a grown man. I shared with you about my son." Then she hugged him and in that moment *everything changed*. When Oshea was released from prison, Mary became a mother figure and mentor to Oshea. She created an organization called "From Death to Life," that allows the families of victims of violence to heal and reconcile.

Mary did the unthinkable. She made a change from the norm of hatred and un-forgiveness and gave forgiveness, hope and a future. Albert Einstein is credited with the quote, "Insanity is doing the same thing repeatedly but expecting a different result." Employing the same attitude and actions of the past, will produce the same results in the present and future. As you renew your mind, know this, nothing changed, nothing new experienced. Newness is hidden in the abundance behind the known. While changes can be difficult, they are necessary.

Like Mary, the Apostle Paul and Silas did the unthinkable after being beaten and imprisoned. According to Acts 16:25-34: "And at midnight Paul and Silas prayed, and sang praises unto God: and the prisoners heard them. And suddenly there was a great earthquake, so that the foundations of the prison were shaken: and immediately all the doors were opened, and every one's bands were loosed." Who prays and sings after being beaten and incarcerated? They made the change and had new experiences. Their freedom was locked to their change.

ASSIGNMENT

That new experience you desire will come from a change. What will you change?

Document your responses to the assignment as well as your challenges and victories.

NEXT

MIND RENEWAL TRANSFORMATION DEVOTIONAL

NEXT

Day 30
LEAVE

Scripture Focus: Genesis 25:29-34

In August 2014, Camille Preston wrote the following in the Fortune magazine

Building good fences—setting boundaries—is one of the most important skills to master for both personal and professional growth. And one of the most important, activities and engagements that we do not enjoy or that do not advance us personally or professionally. When you say no to the things that don't help you, you are, in effect, saying yes to the things that will. By saying no, you open the space necessary for yes. https://fortune.com/2014/08/19/why-saying-no-gets-you-ahead/

That space is very vital to you maximizing your full potential. A quick yes can act as a future shutter. You can easily accept that which is good while blocking your best. The good has the potential to deceive you in believing that you have arrived at your pinnacle, while the best stares at you with desire. A sad reality is, in our haste to be successful, we have settled for good without pursuing best.

This was evident in the account of Genesis 25. Esau was hungry and asked his brother for food. His hunger was so severe, he felt as though he was dying. Jacob, his brother, proposed a barter. Food for birthright. Esau said, "Yes." Jacob fed him and then Esau hated his birth right. Esau by saying yes to his brother Jacob, closed the door to benefiting from his own birth right. The hunger he endured pushed him to settling for good but relinquishing his best. Let us renew our minds with this truth: *you must leave room for the best by saying no to the good.*

ASSIGNMENT

Ask the question, is this the best? If the verdict is no, appreciate but don't settle. Be forever in your pursuit of the best.

Document your responses to the assignment as well as your challenges and victories.

_____

_____

_____

MIND RENEWAL TRANSFORMATION DEVOTIONAL

MIND RENEWAL TRANSFORMATION DEVOTIONAL

CONCLUSION

You are as wealthy as your mind allows you to be. Your mind is the vehicle that drives your success or failure. You will never be successful if your mind registers you as a failure. As you continue to transform your mind with the Word of God, please be conscious that mind renewal is not an event but a journey.

The Bible tells us, with our minds we serve God; Romans 7:25. Therefore If your mind is located at a place of dysfunctionalities, your service unto God will reflect such. It is therefore imperative that a deep mind consultation must be immediately put into effect to ascertain if your mind is conforming to the world or transforming to the mind of Christ. The time has come for you to elevate in mind position.

The real transformation is not in acquiring the mind renewal information but the conversion of thoughts and actions as impacted by the new knowledge received. Use Volume Two alongside the *Mind Renewal* Book. It has five parts which cover topics dealing with issues such as letting the change start with you, finding wealth in service, living a purpose-driven life, dealing with scars and preparation for your "next."

These thirty-day transformational devotional series come equipped with stories, Scriptures, assignments and journal page for documentation. One of the powers of the devotionals is embedded in the assignments given. They are designed to foster the needed change of greater thinking which will produce a wealthier and better you. Be reminded that "faith without works is dead" (James 2:20). The devotionals are the commencement you working out your faith.

ACKNOWLEDGEMENTS

To the Holy Spirit my primary Destiny Helper. I was almost finished writing *Mind Renewal: Biblical Secrets to a Better You*, when you said to me early one morning, "Devotional." I was a bit disappointed because I had an unfinished manuscript that I wanted to complete. I obeyed and here we are today. Thank you for being my guide.

Special thanks to my supportive wife Sherene Morrison, who worked without reservation in editing and proofreading. Your support is invaluable.

Laura Badjnaut, I appreciate you. You willingly gave of your time to fine-tune the manuscript.

My friend Hillary Campbell, you ensured I wrote this book. Your encouragement is priceless. I pray every author finds an encourager like you.

A big thank you to the three readers who willingly gave praise reports: Mrs. Wendy Lawson Stephens, Rev. Ramon Douglas and Mrs. Monique Anderson Coke.

To the team at Extra MILE Innovators, you have certainly lived up to your name. You have gone the extra mile without complaint. Thank you.

ABOUT THE AUTHOR

Jamaican born, Rev. Leostone Peron Morrison, is the author of the book, *Mind Renewal: Biblical Secrets to a Better You,* from which this devotional series was birthed. He has served as an Assistant Pastor and Guidance Counselor at the Ministry of Education in Jamaica. Currently, he is a Probation Officer in St Kitts and Nevis.

Rev. Morrison is the founder of Next Level Let's Climb Bible Study Ministry. Bathroom cleaning was his first ministry assignment.

He is a graduate of the Jamaica Theological Seminary and holds a bachelor's degree in Theology, with a minor in Guidance and Counseling. He acquired a diploma in Biblical Principles from Victory Bible School, and a certificate from the International Accelerated Missions School. Rev. Morrison is married and has four sons and one daughter.

MIND RENEWAL TRANSFORMATION DEVOTIONAL

NOTE: For feedback, consultation or speaking engagements contact Rev. Morrison at restorativeauthor@gmail.com. Kindly submit a review on Amazon or the platform where you bought this book. Thank you.

www.ingramcontent.com/pod-product-compliance
Lightning Source LLC
Chambersburg PA
CBHW060834050426
42453CB00008B/686